COMPLIMENTS OF

To Grow...It's Our Nature

BRITISH
COLUMBIA

Sunset, surf and gull, Pacific Rim National Park

Overleaf: **Lake O'Hara, Yoho National Park**

BRITISH
COLUMBIA
DOUGLAS LEIGHTON

ALTITUDE

Canadian Rockies/Vancouver

PUBLICATION INFORMATION

Canadian Cataloguing in Publication Data
Leighton, Douglas, 1953-
British Columbia
ISBN 1-55153-146-1 Long Beach Cover
ISBN 1-55153-148-8 Okanagan Orchard Cover
ISBN 1-55153-149-6 Bugaboo Mountain Cover
1. British Columbia – Pictorial Works. I. Title.
FC3812.L44 1998   971.1′04′0222   C97-910768-7
F1087.8.L44 1998

Production

Design and art direction	Stephen Hutchings
Editing	Sabrina Grobler & Stephen Hutchings
Electronic page layout	Sharon Komori & Kelly Stauffer
Financial management	Laurie Smith
Sales management	Scott Davidson

Dedication
To my wife, Myriam,
who so patiently waited for the light.

Made in Western Canada
Printed and bound in Western Canada by Friesen Printers, Altona, Manitoba.

Altitude GreenTree Program
Altitude Publishing will plant, in Canada, twice as many trees
as were used in the manufacturing of this book.

Altitude Publishing Canada Ltd.
The Canadian Rockies
1500 Railway Avenue, Canmore, Alberta T1W 1P6

Vineyards, Okanagan Valley, south of Okanagan Falls

CONTENTS

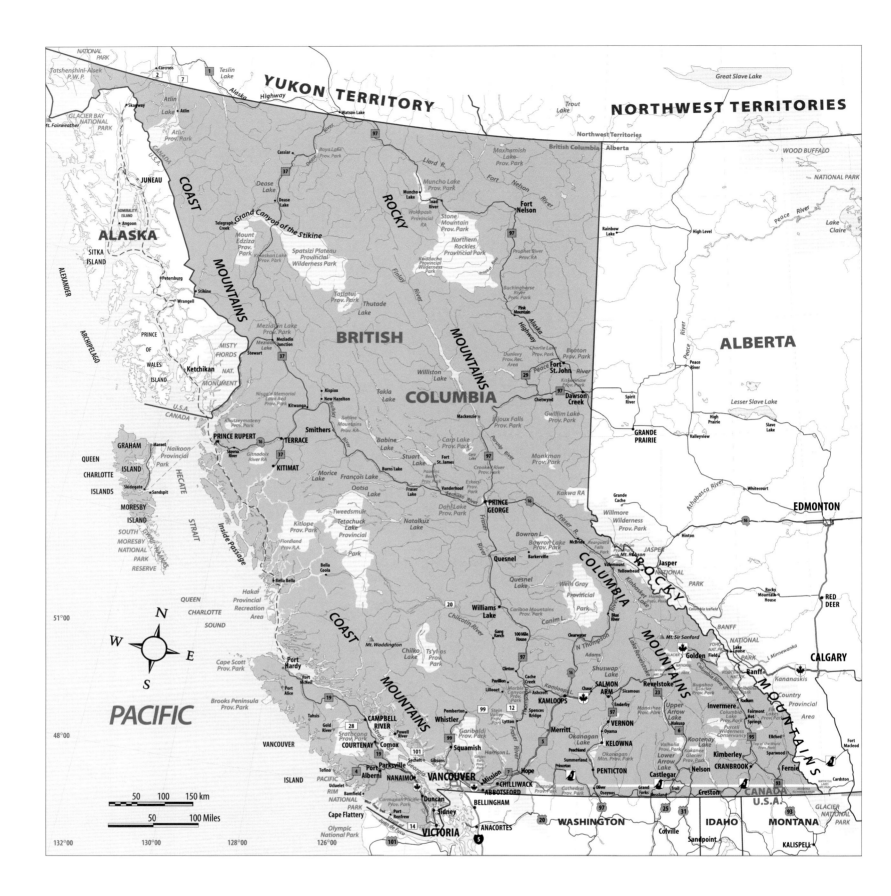

THE PACIFIC PROVINCE

IMAGINE BRITISH COLUMBIA. It is easy to find Canada's third largest province on a map; it looms large on the north Pacific coast between Alaska and Washington state. Visualizing a single image of the province, however, is more challenging.

Many people picture misty fjords and islands, evergreen mountains rising snow-capped out of the Pacific, fishing boats, whales, bald eagles and rivers of salmon. Others imagine the garden cities and farms on the south coast, where 70% of the province's 3.8 million residents live on just 3% of the land.

Just a few hours' drive east of this lush plenitude are hot, dry sagebrush and cactus valleys with irrigated orchards and vast, warm lakes. Farther east, more lakes reflect the grandeur of the Columbia Mountains and the Canadian Rockies. A gold-rush route leads to the "Wild West" in the Cariboo-Chilcotin; a fur-trade route heads north to the Peace River and from Dawson Creek; the Alaska Highway rolls across the vast North Woods and the tundra summits of the northern Rockies. In the northwest, B.C.'s highest mountains soar above vast icefields—a far cry from the garden cities.

Even beyond what one might expect in a province so vast—948,600 km²/366,255 square miles—British Columbia is a place of extraordinary natural diversity. The land itself is a 200-million-year-old mosaic built of geologically distinct "terranes" of the earth's crust, piled randomly onto the ancestral continental shore. This shore has buckled to form the Rockies.

The mild, moist air from the Pacific takes a roller-coaster ride over B.C.'s north-south ranges, creating west-slope wet belts and sunny rainshadows, arctic summits and lush, warm valleys. This mountain-shaped climate makes B.C. the most biologically diverse province in the country with many natural communities and species unique in Canada as well as a few found nowhere else in the world.

B.C.'s many natural communities also supported an equally extraordinary cultural diversity. The province is home to seven of Canada's eleven native linguistic groups, including six First Nations found only here. The earliest recorded European contact was in 1774, when Spanish mariners looking for the Northwest Passage found the Queen Charlotte Islands (Gwaii Haanas) instead. Captain Cook, Britain's "Great Navigator," came next in 1788, mooring at Nootka Sound on Vancouver Island. He sailed away with sea otter pelts, which sparked the first Pacific Rim trade boom when they hit the Chinese market. This trade lured explorer Alexander Mackenzie to the Pacific coast in 1793, when he made the celebrated first historic crossing of the continent.

In 1871, B.C. joined Canada on the promise of a transcontinental railway link to the distant eastern centres. In 1887 the Canadian Pacific Railway train from Montreal chugged into the brand new city of Vancouver and the CPR's S.S. *Abyssinia* from Hong Kong and Yokohama steamed into its new port. The "Fastest Route from Europe to the Orient" had begun and so had B.C.'s coming-of-age on the Pacific Rim.

DOUGLAS LEIGHTON

Overleaf: **Cathedral Grove, MacMillan Provincial Park near Port Alberni**

VICTORIA AND THE PACIFIC RIM

Surfer, Long Beach, Pacific Rim National Park Reserve

Although the big breakers and sand of Canada's "Surf City" may look like California, these waters are Canadian. The hardy surfers, windsurfers and surf kayakers here wear insulating wetsuits, braving even winter storms to ride the wildest waves.

Left: **Wickaninnish Centre, Pacific Rim National Park Reserve**

Parks Canada's centre was named for the Nootka chief who encountered the first Europeans in this area. It overlooks the boundless sunsets, sand and surf of the 10-km/6-mile Long Beach. The mountains of Clayoquot Sound rise majestically in the distance.

VICTORIA AND THE PACIFIC RIM

WINDING OVER 27,000 km (16,500 miles) of rocky shore, British Columbia's Pacific Rim is one of the most rugged and convoluted coastlines in the world. The glacier-draped Coast Mountains march right into the ocean, only to resurface offshore as rocky reefs and islands. The Queen Charlotte Islands off the North Coast and Vancouver Island are the summits of a separate, northbound tectonic plate which occasionally quakes the coast as it grinds by the mainland.

B.C.'s misty coast is one of the Pacific's most fertile shores. When Britain's Captain Cook arrived in 1778, this land-of-plenty supported some of the world's wealthiest aboriginal peoples. Mooring for a month to refit his ships at Nootka Sound on the west coast of Vancouver Island, Cook met the Nootka or Nuu-chah-nulth First Nation at their summer village of Yquot, or Friendly Cove. He discovered that they were a very sophisticated society, lived comfortably in cedar-plank houses and generously distributed gifts, including superbly crafted and decorated artifacts and art, in order to demonstrate their social status.

The fur-trade boom that swept the coast after Cook's visit was almost over by 1843 when Sir James Douglas, the "Father of British Columbia," chose Fort Victoria as the Hudson Bay Company headquarters. In the rolling oak meadows around its harbour, he found "a perfect Eden" that looked and felt like his native English countryside. However, the 1858 Fraser River gold rush saw 25,000 fortune-seekers pass through the small town of 300. By the next year, Victoria had grown tenfold, becoming the colonial capital of Vancouver Island.

Even then, people came for the lifestyle. When the province joined Canada in 1871, members of the governing class chose Victoria as their capital for the good life it would offer them and their distinguished visitors. Today, this "good life" is evident in almost every port on the coast. Moored beside the working fishing boats and timber tugs are sailboats and yachts, sport-fishing skiffs and cruisers, zodiacs filled with scuba gear, sea kayaks and racing sculls.

The BC Ferries are the marine link between the coastal ports on the mainland, Vancouver Island, the Gulf Islands and the remote communities of the central coast. Sailing up the spectacular Inside Passage to Prince Rupert, they become mini cruise ships, passing wild marine parks, bald eagles, pods of orcas and stunning scenery cloaked in evergreen. The southern tip of the Queen Charlotte Islands, became the Gwaii Haanas National Park Reserve and Haida Heritage Site in 1988, protecting rich coasts and Haida archaeological sites. Notable among them is Anthony Island, a UNESCO World Heritage Site that boasts the totems of Sgan Gwaii.

British Columbia's coast has always been famous for its giant trees and old-growth rainforests. Carmanah Pacific Provincial Park adjoining Pacific Rim National Park holds the world's tallest (95 m/317-foot) Sitka spruce, Canada's tallest tree. Kitlope Provincial Park preserves the largest virgin watershed on the central coast, and the great forests of Khutzeymateen Provincial Park north of Prince Rupert are home to both grizzly bears and the unique Kermode bear, a white-coloured black bear.

Right: **British Columbia Parliament Buildings, Victoria**

Empress Hotel, Inner Harbour, Victoria

Opened in 1908 as a premier destination on the Canadian Pacific Railway's "Europe-to-the-Orient" rail and steamship line, the grand "Old Lady" still puts the "British" in British Columbia. Its famous Tea Lobby, the Crystal Ballroom, the Bengal Room, the red "London" double decker buses and the horse-drawn "Tallyhos" all testify to Victoria's historical roots.

Left: **Totems at Thunderbird Park, Victoria**

Displayed here is the work of six distinct peoples: the Haida of the Queen Charlotte Islands, the Tsimshian of the north coast, the Bella Coola and Kwakwaka'wakw of the central coast, the Salish of the Gulf of Georgia and the Nuu-chah-nulth (Nootka) of the west coast of Vancouver Island. Coastal B.C. was the most culturally diverse region in prehistoric Canada.

Victoria Golf Course, Juan de Fuca Strait

Already challenging enough to be ranked one of the top ten courses in Canada, this one provides ocean views across to Washington's Olympic Mountains that are enough to distract even the most serious golfers. The Trial Islands Ecological Reserve offshore preserves B.C.'s greatest concentration of rare and endangered plant species.

Left: **The Butchart Gardens near Victoria**

The Sunken Garden, a limestone quarry transformed into a floral kaleidoscope of living colour, is the centrepiece of these fantastic formal gardens. They began growing in 1904 when Jennie Foster Butchart set to the task of making her oceanside estate beautiful while her husband, concrete pioneer Robert Pim Butchart, mined it. Today, it is among the wonders of the horticultural world.

Ruckle Provincial Park, Saltspring Island

This oceanside park began as Henry Ruckle's homestead in 1872, growing into a 400 ha/1,000-acre mixed farm by 1892. While it has been a park since 1978, part of it is still farmed by Ruckle family members. The original family home, barns, gardens, fruit trees and sheep of all colours exemplify the pastoral seaside charm of the Gulf Islands.

Left: **Montague Harbour Provincial Marine Park, Galiano Island**

Shell Beach, white with crushed and bleached mussel shells, was a natural site for Salish villages. Below the beach, B.C.'s first marine park protects ancient aboriginal settlements that are now submerged in the sea. Above the beach stand orange-barked arbutus trees, the beautiful signature tree of southern Gulf of Georgia shorelines.

Previous page: **BC Ferry in Active Pass from Bluff Park, Galiano Island**

**Ancient Western Red Cedar,
Meares Island in Clayoquot Sound, near Tofino**

Giant trees dwarf visitors to these astonishing old-growth rainforests. Meares Island is home to the world's largest living cedar, the massive trunk of which is 18.5 m/61 feet in circumference.

Left: **Lennard Island Lighthouse, Tofino, Clayoquot Sound**

Once an isolated fishing port on a remote and dangerous coast, Tofino is now an internationally renowned eco-tourism destination that services Pacific Rim National Park Reserve and Clayoquot Sound. The lighthouse dates back to the days when this rough and rocky coast was reputed to be the "Graveyard of the Pacific."

Adult Bald Eagle, Towering Sitka Spruce

Threatened elsewhere in North America, the bald eagle is a common but exciting sight on B.C.'s coast. These opportunistic hunters catch everything from salmon to seabirds, and spend so much time scavenging that some call them E-gulls. Because it takes 4-5 years to achieve this distinctive adult plumage, the dark and mottled juveniles are sometimes mistaken for golden eagles.

Right: **Long Beach, Pacific Rim National Park Reserve**

Canada's first national park on the Pacific Coast was founded in 1970. The 513 km²/198-square-mile park's three units—Long Beach, the Broken Group Islands and the West Coast Trail—stretch along 125 km/80 miles of wild coast. Flocks of small shorebirds and pods of huge Pacific grey whales migrate past this coast each year.

Mural at Chemainus

Afarming area since the 1850s, Chemainus later became a timber town until the mill suddenly shut down in the 1980s. Art saved the town when the downtown was transformed into an outdoor, outsized gallery. Thirty-two vibrant murals depicting the region's colourful history have become a popular tourist attraction.

Left: **April Farms, Comox Valley, Vancouver Island Mountains**

This area has much to offer: one can fish, golf, garden and beachcomb all year round. Vancouver Island's best skiing is on Mt. Washington and the Forbidden Plateau in Strathcona Provincial Park. It is no wonder that this has become B.C.'s fastest-growing region.

Hoodoo, Tribune Bay Provincial Park, Hornby Island

The strange sandstone formations of the shoreline inspire the many potters and artists who live on Hornby Island and the neighbouring Denman Island. The shallow, Caribbean-blue water and white sand beaches have made this sheltered bay a popular summer resort since 1928. Tribune Bay became a provincial park in 1978.

Black Oystercatcher

This crow-sized shorebird is conspicuous on rocky headlands and harbours along the coast; its loud, ringing calls are audible even above the thundering surf. Despite its name, it rarely tackles tough oysters, but finds easier meals in the bountiful, intertidal smorgasbord that clings to the rocks. As the Haida say, "When the tide is out, the table is set."

Orca, Cruise Ship, Inside Passage, near Port McNeil

Cruise ship passengers and whale-watching tours thrill to the sight of orcas in Johnstone Strait. Pods of orcas concentrate here to feed on the massive runs of salmon that funnel through on their way back to the Fraser River. This surge of salmon lures anglers too, making Campbell River (at the south end of the strait) a legendary spot in sportfishing circles.

Right: **Rainforest, Tow Hill Ecological Reserve, Queen Charlotte Islands**

This ancient forest of old-growth Sitka spruce and western red cedar grows on sand dunes along the misty north shore of Graham Island—one of the few sites on the Queen Charlotte Lowlands that is dry enough for such forests to grow. Scientists studying these forest canopies are discovering new species among the mossy branches.

K'una(Skedans) Haida Heritage Site, Louise Island, Haida Gwaii

A village of up to 30 cedar longhouses, each with a carved heraldic pole representing the status and story of its clan, once lined this beach off the east coast of Moresby Island. Access to these fragile sites just north of Gwaii Haanas National Park Reserve is carefully managed by the Haida Watchmen.

Left: Naikoon Provincial Park, Haida Gwaii (Queen Charlotte Islands)

At the top of Tow Hill, the 100 m/300-foot outcrop of basalt columns rising above Agate Beach commands an impressive ocean view. It overlooks the vast bogs and forests of this wild and windswept park on the north-east tip of Graham Island.

Nisga'a Memorial Lava Bed Park, north of Terrace

Nisga'a First Nations history recalls the lives and villages that were lost here 250 years ago when a volcano erupted and poured molten lava into the Nass Valley, igniting rainforests and turning rivers to steam. Now carpeted in mosses, lichens and rock flowers, this vast moonscape contrasts sharply with the lush coastal forests that surround it.

Right: **Ksan Historical Village Museum, Hazelton**

Located on a strategic site at the confluence of two salmon-rich rivers, the Skeena and Bulkley, Ksan is a superbly recreated Gitksan (Tsimshian) First Nations village and a living museum. Here, young artists and performers learn the traditions of their culture from master craftsmen and elders.

VANCOUVER AND
THE LOWER MAINLAND

Vancouver Skyline, English Bay and the North Shore Mountains

Vancouver's unique juxtaposition of urban and natural environments makes it a world-renowned destination. Forming a backdrop to this state-of-the-art city are the North Shore Mountains, a wilderness that stretches to Alaska.

Left: **Nitobe Memorial Gardens, Vancouver**

This traditional Japanese tea garden adjacent to the University of British Columbia, the Dr. Sun Yat-Sen Classical Chinese Garden downtown, the Van-Dusen Botanical Gardens and Queen Elizabeth Park's Bloedel floral garden display various facets of Vancouver's "garden" culture.

VANCOUVER AND THE LOWER MAINLAND

I F THERE is a single image which comes close to defining British Columbia, it may well be the view from the beaches on the west side of Vancouver. This vantage point reveals English Bay, the city's downtown core and the North Shore Mountains. Here, the modern world is located in the midst of the coast's natural endowments: the ocean, the mountains, the evergreen forests.

Greater Vancouver, with its population of 1.8 million and counting, is one of the fastest-growing regions on the continent. The largest port on the west coast and an international financial centre, "Hollywood North" has become a major player on the booming Pacific Rim. An atypical Canadian climate combined with typical Canadian multiculturalism makes Vancouver a home of choice for global villagers. They can talk to Tokyo or London during office hours, sail on English Bay or ski above the city after work and take days off exploring new islands or the ski and snowboard runs at Whistler, one of the world's great ski destinations. In the city, the vibrant, lively downtown is bordered by the waterfront cafés and markets of False Creek, the beaches of the West End and Stanley Park's Seawall, shores and towering trees. The city also offers a cosmopolitan nightlife: NHL or NBA games, opera, night clubs, theatre and a world of restaurants.

Vancouver's recent graduation to the world stage began with Expo '86, a spectacularly successful world's fair held on the city's 100th birthday. The close proximity of the mountains and the ocean contributed significantly to this exciting event, and outside the fairgrounds, the city spoke for itself. When that long, sunny summer shattered the "rainy Vancouver" myth, it seemed that the world decided to move to this new star on the Pacific Rim. While some long-time residents are alarmed by the astonishing rate at which the city is growing, it seems evident in hindsight that its emergence was just a matter of time.

As long ago as 1792, Captain George Vancouver wrote that settlement in the area would "render it the most lovely country that can be imagined," a statement with which Canadian Pacific Railway manager William Cornelius Van Horne concurred when he chose this spectacular harbour for the line's brand new Pacific port. He saw that Vancouver's natural beauty would be a key part of the CPR's "Europe-to-the-Orient" appeal for tourists. When the city was incorporated in 1886, one of its council's first acts was to establish Stanley Park, which enthralled visitors boarding CPR steamships to the Orient and still delights cruise-ship passengers to Alaska today.

Greater Vancouver sprawls south and east across the delta and lower valley of the Fraser River, which churns out of the interior carrying the silt that results in some of Canada's richest farmlands. Once threatened by floods, the lower Fraser valley is now a garden, and the dairy farms below the snow-capped mountains of Abbotsford and Chilliwack exemplify this area's serenity.

Right: **Grouse Mountain, North Vancouver**

Symphony of Fire over English Bay

This spectacular summer event is visible from high points all around the city. Hundreds of thousands of spectators seek the best views from the beaches around English Bay and make a party of it.

Left: **English Bay Beaches, West End, North Shore Mountains**

The West End was developed a century ago as the city's finest residential district. Adjacent to Stanley Park, it is lined with sandy beaches.

Canada Place, Cruise Ship Sailing past Stanley Park

Originally built for Canada's Expo '86 pavilion, the stylized Teflon sails of Canada Place on Burrard Inlet have become a city trademark. Now a port for Alaska-bound cruise ships, the former Pier BC served the CPR's Pacific Empress liners, which sailed to the Orient a century ago.

Right: **Downtown, Coal Harbour from Stanley Park Seawall**

Stanley Park is the pride of Vancouver. Surrounded by beaches and rocky headlands, it holds giant-tree forests, lakes, colourful totems, cricket fields, playgrounds and the Vancouver Aquarium. The spectacular Seawall surrounds the park, offering a panoramic view of the city, ocean and mountains.

Chinatown Market, East Pender Street

Vancouver's Pacific Rim roots are most vividly displayed in this downtown neighborhood. Although the large Chinese community is now spread throughout Greater Vancouver, its members still frequent this district's shopping and dining centre. Chinese pioneers first came to B.C. in the 1858 gold rush.

Left: **False Creek Harbour**

After a day on English Bay, many Vancouverites dock their boats and walk home. Along False Creek, a brand new waterfront community is growing on the Expo '86 lands.

Vancouver from the British Properties, West Vancouver

Vancouver's famous Lion's Gate Bridge, which spans Burrard Narrows, was completed in 1938. It was intended to connect the first phase of the "super-view" residential district, developed by Britain's famous Guinness brewing (and now "World Record") family. At dusk, the dark forests of Stanley Park are silhouetted against the bright downtown lights.

Left: **Vancouver, Burrard Inlet from North Vancouver**

Reminiscent of the steep streets of San Francisco, this view down Lonsdale extends across Burrard Inlet to Canada Place downtown. The SeaBuses crossing the inlet carry many rush-hour commuters who are delighted to avoid the ever-busier bridges.

Horseshoe Bay Ferry, Howe Sound

British Columbia Ferries are part of life on the coast. From this West Vancouver port, they sail to Vancouver Island, the Sunshine Coast and Bowen Island. For some islanders, it's a relaxing daily commute; for visitors, it's a mini ocean cruise.

Right: **Whistler Village, Blackcomb Mountain**

Established as the province's first and only Resort Municipality in 1975, Whistler was developed with the help of famous B.C. Olympic skier Nancy Greene. It is now consistently rated North America's top ski resort. The village sits at the base of two huge mountains, Whistler and Blackcomb, which boast the longest runs on the continent. Locals spend the summers on beautiful golf courses and hiking trails that lead into the adjacent Garibaldi Provincial Park.

Snow Geese at the Reifel Bird Sanctuary, Ladner

The Fraser Delta is a vital rest and feeding stop for millions of waterfowl and shorebirds migrating on the Pacific Flyway. The myriad flocks of white, honking snow geese coming to and from Siberia are a breathtaking spectacle.

Left: **Annieville Fishing Port, Fraser River, Surrey**

Each year millions of salmon swim up the Fraser through Greater Vancouver, making their way past the boats that are trying to catch them. Down river, the heritage village of Steveston is the site of the giant Gulf of Georgia Cannery which operated from 1894 to 1979 and is now a National Historic Site. Steveston still hosts a "fresh from the boat" dockside fish market.

Fraser Valley, near Chilliwack

Aptly named "Rainbow Country," this valley is squeezed between the Coast and Cascade Mountains, where the weather often breaks. This combination of coastal moisture and hot Interior sun results in an abundance of farm produce on the fertile Fraser River bottomlands. Lush forests and waterfalls drape the rugged slopes that rise abruptly from the fields.

Right: **Trumpeter Swans, Fraser Valley, near Agassiz**

Reflected here in Maria Slough near Agassiz, the snow-capped 2,107 m/6,913-foot Cheam Peak in the Cascade Mountains is one of the most prominent landmarks in the Fraser Valley. Once almost extinct, these huge swans—the largest North American waterfowl—are once again a familiar winter sight on the south coast.

THOMPSON-OKANAGAN

Pocket Desert Ecological Reserve, north of Osoyoos Lake

Preserving a small parcel of the South Okanagan's edge of the Great Basin Desert, this reserve features savannahs of greasewood shrubs: the floral signature of this unique ecosystem. Famous for its rattlesnakes, scorpions and pricklypear cacti, this beautiful desert is a national treasure.

Left: **Helmcken Falls, Wells Gray Provincial Park**

Helmcken Falls, Canada's fourth-highest waterfall, occurs when the pristine Murtle River takes a 137 m/450-foot plunge over the edge of an ancient lava bed. Most of Wells Gray Provincial Park, an enormous 5,297 km²/2,045-square-mile wilderness park, is the headwaters of the North Thompson River.

THOMPSON-OKANAGAN

I N SOUTHWESTERN B.C. on the sunny side of the Coast and Cascade mountains are the Okanagan and Thompson valleys, often referred to as "Canada's California." In the valleys, the winters are often short and moderate while the long, hot summers seem to last forever. The peach orchards, vineyards and beach culture surrounding the warm lakes can indeed invoke images of California—in quieter times.

These big grassland valleys, cut deeply into the forested highlands of the Interior Plateau, are among B.C.'s driest areas; the south Okanagan comes as close to a true desert as any landscape in Canada. The sun and water also create B.C.'s best beach resorts on Kalamalka, Okanagan, Skaha and Osoyoos lakes in the Okanagan and Shuswap Lake in the Thompson. The small lakes on the highlands, native home of the high-jumping Kamloops rainbow trout, are every fly fisher's dream.

The Salish people who first inhabited the Okanagan hunted, gathered wild produce and made rock paintings at places they called Kelowna, Penticton and Osoyoos, while those around Kamloops also feasted on the huge runs of big Pacific salmon in the Thompson River. Aboriginal heritage sites here date back 7,500 years.

The Okanagan valley was explored in 1811 by David Stuart, an American fur trader who headed north to establish Fort Kamloops, the first white settlement in southern B.C. By 1858, pioneering ranchers were pushing cattle north through Osoyoos, and Fort Kamloops thrived as a cowtown, supplying beef to the Cariboo goldfields.

The Canadian Pacific Railway arrived in 1885 and soon brought the first international tourists to the CPR's Hotel Sicamous on Shuswap Lake. The rails reached Okanagan Lake in 1893 and headed south to Penticton, where the first commercial orchards had already been planted. This fruit belt had been discovered by white people in the 1860s, and by 1900, more than a million fruit trees grew there. The orchards expanded even more when the irrigation projects of the 1920s turned the parched southern valley green.

Today, the valley produces 30% of Canada's apples, 100% of its apricots, 60% of its cherries, 20% of its peaches and 50% of its pears and plums, not to mention some outstanding wine. Free-trade competition has brought out the very best in Okanagan vintners in recent years; small, creative wineries are now producing award-winning vintages to rival the world's best. During the valley-wide wine festivals that take place every fall, the local wine-makers celebrate the fruits of their labours.

Since it was connected directly to the Lower Mainland by the Coquihalla Highway in 1986, the Thompson-Okanagan region has welcomed an increasing number of new residents who are drawn to the area's climate and lifestyle. The growing centres of Kelowna, Penticton, Vernon, Kamloops and Salmon Arm are vibrant towns which offer a multitude of attractions: lakes, fruit stands and golf courses galore; trails such as the one to the canyons of Okanagan Mountain; the alpine summits of Cathedral Lakes; and the vast wilderness of Wells Gray. To help make the most of winter, there's lots of powder skiing at Sun Peaks, Silver Star, Big White and Apex resorts as well as long cross-country trails on the surrounding highlands.

Right: **Village of Chase, Little Shuswap and Shuswap Lakes, South Thompson River Valley**

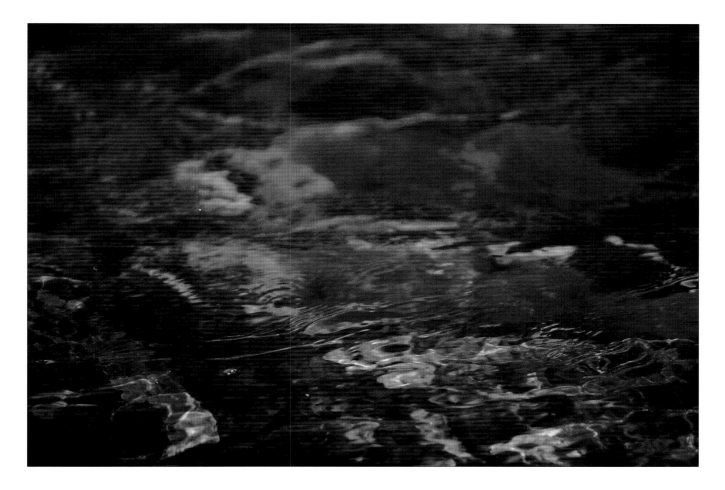

Sockeye Salmon, Adams River, east of Chase

One of B.C.'s largest salmon runs occurs just off the TransCanada Highway in the Shuswap area. Pushing 485 km/300 miles up the Fraser and South Thompson rivers, sockeye return every fall to spawn. In peak years, millions of fish crowd the 11 km/7-mile river and thousands of visitors can see them during the "Salute to the Sockeye" in Roderick Haig-Brown Provincial Park.

Left: **Little River, above Little Shuswap Lake**

The Little River runs between Shuswap and Little Shuswap Lake east of Chase. Because bears were once abundant here, the Salish people called this place *Squilax*, or "black bear," which are attracted by the autumn salmon runs. Anglers cast for salmon and big trout in the valley rivers and lakes and for small "Kamloops" rainbow trout in the many lakes on the surrounding plateaus.

Bounding Mule Deer Fawn near Vernon

The Okanagan's mild, dry valleys are ideal winter range for mule deer. They descend from their summer pastures in the high country, much to the dismay of fruit growers who must fence the animals away from their fruit trees.

Left: **Stormy Sunset, Shuswap Lake, Monashee Mountain Foothills**

The evening sun sets on the Salmon Arm, the southernmost arm of the huge, H-shaped Shuswap Lake. Shuswap Lake is the houseboat capital of western Canada, thanks in large part to the lack of private cottages, the 1,000 km/625 miles of shoreline, the 20 marine-access parks and the warm lake water during the summer season.

Okanagan Lake Beach, Penticton

Located between the beautiful beaches on Okanagan and Skaha Lakes, Penticton was a summer holiday destination even before the first tourists arrived by sternwheeler in 1893. The S.S. *Sicamous*, which plied the waters of Okanagan Lake from 1914 to 1935, has been beached here since 1951. Penticton began in 1865 as the home ranch of Tom Ellis, "Cattle King of the Okanagan."

Left: **Kelowna, Okanagan Lake from Knox Mountain Park**

This fertile plain was home to the Okanagan's first European settlement; Father Charles Pandosy's 1860 mission planted the valley's first apples and vineyards. Since the Coquihalla Connector opened Kelowna to the Lower Mainland in 1988, the city has rapidly become the largest centre in the Interior. The famous floating bridge was opened in 1958.

Vineyards above Okanagan Falls

Creative Okanagan vintners have recently established a strong international reputation for the high quality of their local wines. The many vineyards owe their existence to modern irrigation techniques.

Left: **Orchards above Naramata, Okanagan Lake**

The benchlands northeast of Penticton, a rural mosaic of rolling orchards, offer a sweeping vista across the lake to the Giant's Head above Summerland, as well as north to the rocky canyons of Okanagan Mountain Provincial Park and south to Skaha Lake. Together with Peachland (est. 1897) and Summerland (est. 1902), Naramata was founded in 1907 by John Moore Robinson, who loved its name—"Smile of the Manitou"—when he heard it spoken by a Sioux chief in a seance.

Vaseaux Lake, McIntyre Bluff, south of Okanagan Falls

This shallow lake has been a federal bird sanctuary since the 1920s and remains a birder's mecca. It is home to unique semi-desert birds like canyon wrens, white-throated swifts and white-headed woodpeckers. The Vaseaux-Bighorn National Wildlife Area protects this rare habitat and the California bighorn sheep that range here.

Right: **Starry Night above Vaseaux Lake**

The warm Okanagan nights are perfect for stargazing beneath towering Ponderosa pines and Douglas firs. On this October night, the aurora borealis, popularly known as the "Northern Lights," made a rare southern appearance.

Richter Pass, Cascade Mountains, west of Osoyoos

This low pass between the Okanagan and Similkameen valleys, directly in the rain shadow of the Cascade Mountains, traverses some of the most arid rangeland in B.C. Cattle graze in spring pastures surrounded by vast swaths of sagebrush—home of the Sage Thrasher, one of Canada's rarest birds. Cathedral Lakes Provincial Park sits atop the distant snow-capped range.

Left: **Orchards above Osoyoos Lake**

Osoyoos Lake lies just north of the international border. Osoyoos' native Salish name means the "narrowing of the waters." It is Canada's warmest lake. The far (east) side of the lake is home to the Inkaneep Salish First Nation and is the largest portion of the valley's remaining semi-desert.

THE CANADIAN ALPS:
THE KOOTENAYS AND ROCKIES

Sunrise over Mt. Loki, Purcell Mountains, Kootenay Lake

Clouds hover just above the big lakes of the West Kootenays. The region's famous ski mountains rise above this blanket, leaving fields of powder snow beneath sunny skies. In the summer, hang gliders launch from this peak above the town of Kaslo.

Left: "The Monarch," Mt. Robson Provincial Park

Towering above the headwaters of the Fraser River and the Yellowhead Pass, the highest peak in the Canadian Rockies (3,954 m/12,972 feet) catches the last rays of a summer sunset. This challenging peak, frequently covered by clouds, was first climbed in 1913 by an Alpine Club of Canada team led by the renowned Austrian guide Conrad Kain.

THE CANADIAN ALPS: THE KOOTENAYS AND ROCKIES

THE PARKS AND PEAKS of southeastern B.C. (including Canada's "Matterhorn," Mt. Assiniboine, the magnificent Emerald Lake, and the "Great Glacier" above Rogers Pass) are international icons of mountain majesty. Though undeniably breathtaking, their renown is linked to the Canadian Pacific Railway. When the railway arrived in the early 1880s, the CPR encouraged the creation of Yoho and Glacier national parks (complete, of course, with CPR hotels in key locations). Promoted internationally as "The Canadian Alps," these destinations were immediately appealing to travellers.

Yoho National Park is part of the Canadian Rockies, a "young" (75 million years) chain of huge sedimentary rock slabs which have been crushed together and tilted upwards so that now sea-bottom fossils emerge on the tops of the peaks. This "Serengeti of North America" is prime habitat for large mammals: it is home to most of B.C.'s elk, mule and white-tailed deer, Rocky Mountain bighorn sheep, many mountain goats, moose and a few woodland caribou.

To the east of the Canadian Rockies, there are many more caribou, black and grizzly bears in the lush Columbia Mountains—the Selkirk, Purcell, Monashee and Cariboo ranges. The Columbias catch Canada's greatest snowfalls, which irrigate forests and subalpine meadows in the summer but thunder down on the valleys in the form of avalanches in the winter.

While native trails traversed many passes through the Rockies, there were few that led through the Columbias. The Canadian Pacific Railway, however, in search of a route across the southern part of Canada, pushed the rails over previously unused passes. Later, to make the precipitous grades less dangerous, tunnels were bored underneath these two passes: the Spiral Tunnels lie beneath the Kicking Horse Pass in the Rockies, and in the Columbias, Rogers Pass was replaced with what is now North America's longest railway tunnel.

These mountains were natural tourist attractions and parks were quickly established along the railway lines. In 1913, Mt. Robson Provincial Park was established to welcome the Canadian National Railway, and the next year Mt. Revelstoke National Park was created along the CPR route. Then came the first highway park, when the Banff-Windermere Highway opened in 1923 and Kootenay National Park was established along it.

Long a favourite holiday destination, the Rocky Mountain Trench is a quieter alternative to the busy National Parks and offers some special attractions: the world's best heli-skiing in the Columbia Mountains; wild rides down the Kicking Horse, Canada's busiest whitewater-rafting river; and calm hours of wildlife-watching from a canoe in the Columbia Wetlands. Hang-gliders soar to record record-breaking flights down the valley and others take beautiful helicopter rides to mountaintop lodges. Major ski areas run at Panorama near Invermere, above the "Bavarian City" of Kimberley and at Fernie, the new powder capital of the Rockies.

Skiers have discovered the West Kootenays, too. The first Canadian skier to win an Olympic gold medal, Nancy Greene, put her home town of Rossland and its Red Mountain runs on the map. Later, the steep-and-deep powder runs at Whitewater above Nelson began to lure international skiers. When the snow melted, they discovered Canada's quiet, beautiful Switzerland with its garden climate, heritage buildings and great mountain lakes. One of B.C.'s best-kept secrets was out.

**Drinnon Peak, Gwillim Lakes Plateau, Valhalla Provincial Park
near New Denver**

Established in 1983, this 498 km²/192-square-mile wilderness stretches from the beaches along the pristine Slocan Lake up through virgin watersheds to mountain lakes and alpine meadows. The sculpted gneiss peaks of the Valhalla Range, with cliffs that rival Yosemite, have long attracted serious climbers.

Left: **Kootenay Valley Farmlands, Selkirk Mountains, near Creston**

This broad valley above Kootenay Lake between the Selkirk and Purcell Ranges of the Columbia Mountains was once a vast wetland, seasonally flooded with water and waterfowl. Much of this is rich farmland, but portions of the land were saved for wildlife in the Creston Valley Wildlife Management Area. The endangered "Selkirk International" herd of mountain woodland caribou roams the distant mountaintops.

Previous page: **Kootenay Valley Farmlands, Selkirk Mountains,
near Creston**

Grizzly Plaza, Revelstoke

This busy centre is located in the historic downtown area of Revelstoke, a key Canadian Pacific Railway city since 1885. Its restored heritage architecture enhances the beauty of this recreation destination in the heart of the rugged Columbia Mountains.

Left: **Village of Kaslo, Kootenay Lake, Purcell Mountains**

Before the ore ran out, Kaslo was a paddle-wheeler port that supplied the "Silvery Slocan" mines in the mountains via a narrow-gauge railway. The S.S. *Moyie*, a National Historic Site that is now permanently moored in its harbour, was also an important supply link. Long renowned for its trophy rainbow trout fishing, this sleeping beauty has come to life recently as a recreation and retirement centre and a peaceful setting for many computer-linked professionals.

Summit Meadows, Mount Revelstoke National Park

Irrigated by melting snow during long, sunny summers, lush subalpine flower meadows thrive atop the Columbia Mountains. Visitors drive the park road to this 1,830 m/6,000-foot summit in the Selkirk Range, which is the main attraction of this 263 km²/102-square-mile park.

Right: **Selkirk Range above Rogers Pass, Glacier National Park**

Major A.B. Rogers climbed the ridge north of the 3,294 m/10,808-foot Mt. Sir Donald in 1881 to behold "his" pass through the Columbia Mountains. By 1916, the line had been re-routed into the newly constructed 8 km/5-mile Connaught Tunnel located below the snowbound pass. Since 1988 it has run through the 14.6 km/ 9-mile Mt. Macdonald Tunnel, the longest in North America. The Trans-Canada Highway stays open each winter, thanks to preemptive artillery strikes on the avalanche slopes above it.

Heli-skiers, Cariboo Mountains south of Valemount

Heli-skiing was invented in the Columbia Mountains by mountaineering pioneer Hans Gmoser, who started flying powder-lovers to dream runs in the Bugaboo Range (Purcell Mountains) in the 1960s. Boundless terrain and Canada's greatest snowfalls, averaging 14.3 m/47 feet annually at Mt. Fidelity near Rogers Pass, make the Columbia Range a world-famous heli-skiing mecca.

Left: **Rocky Mountaineer Touring Train, Beaver Valley, Glacier National Park**

Recognizing the tourism potential of the awesome mountains along their line, the Canadian Pacific Railway encouraged the reservation of land to establish Glacier and Yoho national parks in 1886. Today, passengers on this independent touring train enjoy these spectacular views.

Rocky Mountain Bighorn Ram

The winter range of these grazers is restricted to the steep, windswept slopes of the Rocky Mountains. Eastbound travellers on the Trans-Canada Highway usually spot the sheep in the Kicking Horse Canyon above the town of Golden.

Left: **Bugaboo Spires, Purcell Mountains, south of Golden**

While these granite towers are now best known by heli-skiing enthusiasts, they've intrigued mountaineers since 1910. The Snowpatch Spire, one of the most technically challenging climbs in the world, wasn't conquered until 1940. These peaks are now within the 253 km²/98-square-mile Bugaboo Glacier Provincial Park. Farther south, the huge Purcell Wilderness Conservancy protects the wild heart of this rugged range of the Columbia Mountains.

Floe Lake, Kootenay National Park

This hiker's basin lies along The Rockwall, a palisade of towering cliffs and peaks on the park's western border. The ice floes that calve off the glacier and float into the lake each summer are usually gone by the time the subalpine larches turn yellow in September.

Left: **Takakkaw Falls, Yoho National Park**

Dropping 378 m/1,240 feet from a glacial basin on the Great Divide, this highest single cascade in Canada fills the Yoho Valley with spray, rainbows and a thundering roar in summer. It falls silent in winter, becoming one of the most challenging ice-climbing routes on the continent. Its Cree name means "it is wonderful."

Bull Elk, Kootenay National Park

Every September, the quiet valleys of the Rockies echo with the eerie bugles of bull elk or wapiti, which broadcast their competition for breeding rights. The Rocky Mountains are home to most of B.C.'s elk.

Right: **Invermere, Lake Windermere, Rocky Mountains**

These warm lakes and hot springs have been holiday destinations for Albertans ever since the Banff-Windermere Highway was finished in 1923. Today, the valley offers golf courses, dude ranches, mountain lodges, white-water rafting and ski hills. In this aerial view northeast to the Rockies, Mt. Assiniboine stands prominently on the Continental Divide.

Fort Steele Heritage Town, Stormy Mt. Fisher

Named in 1888 for the arrival of Superintendent Sam Steele of the North-West Mounted Police, Fort Steele was born during the 1864 Wild Horse Creek gold rush. The town died when the railway bypassed it in favour of Cranbrook in 1898, but has since been restored as a lively re-creation of the town's history.

Right: **Horses Grazing near Moyie Lake**

Wild horses roamed the East Kootenays until the 1960s, grazing lush pastures like this one near the old logging town of Lumberton. The Kutenai Indians of this region were the first in B.C. to obtain horses and were skilled equestrians when explorer David Thompson met them in 1807. The Kutenai sometimes crossed the Rockies to hunt bison in the Alberta foothills.

CARIBOO-CHILCOTIN

Rush Hour on the Gang Ranch

Herding cattle and riding fencelines is still part of the job for many working cowboys on the big Chilcotin ranches, which are spread over country too rugged for roads. This 400,000 ha/1,000,000-acre ranch is the biggest in Canada. Established in the 1860s, it sprawls across the remote west side of the Fraser.

Left: **Nechako River at Fort Fraser**

The first Europeans in the Interior were fur traders who became partners with native peoples in the new trading economy. The Carrier Indians are so named for their traditional role as traders between coast and interior tribes. In 1793, they led Alexander Mackenzie on their overland trail to the Pacific. At this time, he completed the historic, first-recorded crossing of the continent.

CARIBOO-CHILCOTIN

BRITISH COLUMBIA's "Wild West" is the vast Interior Plateau of forests, grasslands and lakes that rolls north of the Thompson Valley and spans the area from the Coast Mountains east to the Rockies. It is part of the watershed of the Fraser River, which carves a great canyon and semi-desert gorge between the remote Chilcotin Plateau to the west and the Cariboo to the east.

Highway travellers miss most of this awesome canyon; most roads, like the historic trails that preceded them, follow a more gentle route east of the river. Millions of spawning salmon have no choice but to swim hard up the canyon and rest in sheltered eddies along the rocky shore. A vital staple for the Salish, Chilcotin and Carrier First Nations living along the Fraser and its tributaries, these salmon were sun-dried, smoked and stored for the winter.

In 1860, prospectors pushed east from Quesnel on the Fraser into the snowy Cariboo Mountain foothills and found the first big nuggets of the fabulous Cariboo Gold Rush. The next spring, one lucky pan yielded an astonishing 2.7 kg (96 ounces) of gold. By 1864, Barkerville, bursting with 10,000 gold rushers, was the biggest town west of Chicago and north of San Francisco.

To feed the gold rushers, some of Canada's largest ranches in Canada were established on the Fraser and Chilcotin grasslands and some, like the giant Gang Ranch, are still operating. Working cowboys still ride these rugged, roadless ranges and celebrate the Wild West at the Williams Lake Stampede, the biggest rodeo in the region. The gold rush was already over by the time the Royal Engineers completed the vital Cariboo Road up the Fraser Canyon to Barkerville in 1865. The road brought a new wave of settlers who spearheaded the forest industry that is now the economic mainstay of the entire region.

Many of the cowboys at Williams Lake come into town on Highway 22, the 480 km (298-mile) road west across the Chilcotin to Bella Coola on the Pacific. Until 1953, this road had a 60 km (37-mile) gap over the Coast Mountains. Tired of government delays, the locals finished the "Freedom Road" themselves.

Today, despite being just a few hours' flight from Vancouver, the Chilcotin remains one of the wildest parts of the province. Highway 22 rivals the Alaska Highway for the spectacular scenery it provides. California bighorn sheep watch rafters and kayakers challenge the river canyons; naturalists watch birds galore in B.C.'s "duck factory" on the plateau. Westward rises the 4,016 m (13,177-foot) Mt. Waddington, the highest peak in the Coast Range. Two huge wilderness parks—the new Ts'yl-os Provincial Park is around glacial Chilko Lake and Tweedsmuir Provincial Park, which straddles the Coast Mountains—are among this route's splendours.

At the guest ranches, fishing lodges and cross-country resorts of the South Cariboo lakelands, the big skies and wide-open spaces still evoke the "Wild West," and enough "colour" still appears in the pans of working and weekend prospectors to keep gold-rush dreams alive.

Right: **Grand Canyon of the Fraser River, north of Lillooet**

Black Bear, Tweedsmuir Provincial Park

Black bear populations flourish in this park, which sprawls across the Coast Range. Here, they find abundant food in the forests and salmon-rich rivers. Mothers with cubs keep especially close to the forest cover, sending their cubs up trees when wolf packs, grizzlies or male black bears threaten them.

Right: **Nemiah Valley, Coast Mountains**

These remote grasslands border the newly created Ts'yl-os Provincial Park, a 2,332 km²/1,449-square-mile wilderness rising to Good Hope Mountain and bordering Chilko Lake. The park is co-managed by the Nemiah Valley First Nation people, who have traditional claims on the valley.

Lac Des Roches, east of 100 Mile House

The high, rolling plateau of the South Cariboo is dappled with lakes teeming with Kamloops rainbow trout. It is home to many fishing resorts, guest ranches and cross-country ski lodges.

Barkerville Gold Rush Town, west of Quesnel

Surrounded by gold strikes, Barkerville became the bustling hub of the Cariboo Gold Rush in 1862, when a stubborn English prospector named Billy Barker started digging while everyone else panned. He hit the motherlode 17 m/52 feet down—just as he'd envisioned in a dream. A Provincial Historic Park since 1958, Barkerville is as lively in summers now as it ever was, but is much quieter on autumn days like this.

**Autumn Bunchberries, McLeod River above War Falls,
Carp Lake Provincial Park**

This 6,000 ha/15,000-acre park north of Prince George boasts rolling forests of pine, spruce and aspen, wetlands, waterfalls and—the main attraction—lakes full of rainbow trout. In 1805, this fishery fed fur traders at the nearby Fort McLeod, the first European settlement west of the Rockies.

Right: **Summer Cow Moose**

A familiar sight in Cariboo forests, lakes and wetlands, these biggest, tallest and homeliest members of the deer family have expanded their range southward over the past 50 years, finding abundant food in forests disturbed by fire and logging.

Northern British Columbia

Spring Avalanche Paths, Bear Pass, near Stewart

The northern spring is impatient; green shoots push out from the edges of these deep snowpacks, still melting at the bottom of avalanche paths. The steep slopes above clear early, creating prime spring pastures for the bears of this aptly-named pass. Later, the bears move to berry patches and salmon rivers for bigger feasts.

Left: **One Island Lake Provincial Park, south of Dawson Creek**

On the northeast slope of Rockies, this remote park offers a first taste of the "true north" with loon calls and long sunsets, lichen-draped spruces and reindeer moss. Forest fire smoke adds rare colours to this sunset sky.

NORTHERN BRITISH COLUMBIA

NORTHERN BRITISH COLUMBIA is a vast land about the size of Germany with more moose than people. Because of the long, frigid winters in the boreal forests of the northeast and the snowbound winters in the mountain west, this last frontier posed huge challenges to explorers and settlers—and still does. In today's crowded world, however, these challenges are eagerly accepted by thousands of adventurers every year who are lured by the promise of discovery.

Northeastern B.C. is a forested plain rolling down from the Continental Divide. Here, rivers run north to the Arctic. With the exception of a sliver of prairie grainbelt that runs along the Peace River, this land is wild. Out of the North Woods came the fur traders, led by Alexander Mackenzie, who paddled up the Peace River in 1792. In 1794, they established Rocky Mountain Fort near Fort St. John, the first white trading post on the B.C. mainland.

Most travellers to the North start from the Peace River region, where the serene and lovely canola fields are punctuated with grain elevators. Most of the North's residents are concentrated in the cities of Fort St. John and Dawson Creek, farm towns turned busy energy and forestry centres.

North of the Peace are boundless forests and muskegs, lakes and slow-winding rivers. In November of 1941, this wilderness was home to isolated native bands, bushplanes and a few hunting and fishing camps. A month later, it became a vital link to Alaska for World War II security. In March of 1942, an army of 11,000 U.S. soldiers, 16,000 civilians and 7,000 heavy machines invaded Dawson Creek, "Mile Zero," and began to forge the 2,400 km (1,500-mile) Alaska Highway through "mountains, muskeg and mosquitoes." They met the northern crews at Mile 1,061 in the Yukon Territory only 9 months later.

To travel the Alaska Highway is to experience one of the great North American road trips. Crossing frost-heaving muskegs, spring-flooding valleys and rock-sliding summits, this road was once notorious for its potholes, flying gravel and mud. Today, it's a paved, well-serviced cruise.

In the remote, sparsely populated mountains are some of B.C.'s largest wilderness parks. In the St. Elias Range in the far northwest, B.C.'s highest peak, the 4,663 m (15,300-foot) Mt. Fairweather, towers above the newly established 9,580 km^2 (3,698-square-mile) Tatshenshini-Alsek Wilderness Provincial Park. Together with Alaska's Glacier Bay National Park and Kluane National Park in the Yukon, this is the continent's largest protected area.

In the Coast Range, Atlin Provincial Park lies between glaciers and Atlin Lake, and Mt. Edziza Provincial Park surrounds an ancient volcano. In the drier Cassiar-Omineca Mountains farther inland, herds of mountain goats, stone sheep and woodland caribou roam the vast highlands of Spatsizi Plateau Wilderness Park. In 1997 B.C. added still more to its wealth of wilderness parks with the creation of the Northern Rocky Mountains Provincial Park southwest of the Alaska Highway.

Most of these parks are accessible only by air or trail, but the 725 km (450-mile) Stewart-Cassiar Highway 37, completed in 1972, runs through the heart of all this wild mountain country. Connecting the Alaska Highway in the Yukon to the Yellowhead Highway (16) on the Skeena River, this route north is becoming increasingly popular.

Right: **Bear Glacier, near Stewart**

Late Sun, Forests above Meziadin Lake

This lush forest, alive with singing birds and munching moose and beaver, stretches below the Stewart-Cassiar Highway. This increasingly popular route north to Alaska rolls along the eastern foothills of the northern Coast Mountains past huge wilderness parks, frontier posts and wildlife galore.

Right: **Tyhee Lake, Bulkley Valley, near Smithers**

In the rain shadow of the heavily forested Hazelton Mountains of the Coast Range, these sunny benchlands above the village of Telkwa are rolling aspen parklands, pastures and farms. Hudson Bay Mountain, dominating the skyline, offers outstanding skiing. The Bulkley River and nearby Babine Lake country are internationally renowned salmon and steelhead waters.

Alaska Highway, north of Pink Mountain

From the Rocky Mountain foothills comes the first of many vast, sweeping views that await travellers on the 2,400 km/1,500-mile Alaska Highway.

Left: **Peace River Valley, west of Fort St. John**

Flowing from the Rocky Mountains on the distant horizon, this great river was a natural route for the first fur traders exploring B.C. from the east. The first trading post, Rocky Mountain Fort, was established near here in 1794. Pioneers found a fertile northern farmbelt here. Today, energy from Peace River dams and fossil fuels, forestry and tourism power this frontier economy.

Sub-adult Grizzly Bear Feeding on Soopolallie Berries

In their third year, grizzly bears leave the security of their mothers and begin fending for themselves. Because they are stressed and often hungry, their erratic behaviour leads researchers to call them "teen-aged" bears. The close family ties between bears and dogs are evident in these lean juveniles—a relationship that explains much about these unpredictable individuals. Just as every dog is different, so is every bear.

Right: **Muncho Lake Provincial Park**

This shoreline service centre and bush-plane port on Muncho Lake—"Big Lake" in the local Kaskan native dialect—is the focal point of activity in this 884 km²/341-square-mile park at the northwestern end of the Rockies. Stone (Dall) sheep live above the lake and are often seen here and at the nearby Stone Mountain Provincial Park, where the Alaska Highway reaches its high point at the 1,295 m/4,249-foot Summit Pass on the Continental Divide.

Bull Woodland Caribou

Attracted by road salt, caribou cows and calves are sometimes seen along the Alaska Highway, especially in the Rockies around Stone Mountain and Muncho Lake Provincial Parks. The bulls, looking just as they are portrayed on the Canadian quarter, are more often seen during the autumn rutting season.

Right: **Liard River Hot Springs Provincial Park**

Although rumours that this was a tropical valley with parrots and monkeys proved to be false, this oasis is exotic enough for the Alaska Highway travellers who savour a dip in the two natural 38-49°C pools, keeping this park busy all summer. A boardwalk (originally constructed by Alaska Highway builders in 1942) crosses this unique ecosystem, which is warmed by the hot springs' outflow.

Aurora Borealis, Alaska Highway near Prophet River

Scientists tell us that the Northern Lights are the visible displays of solar winds washing sub-atomic particles through the Earth's magnetic field. Aboriginal people saw the spirits of their ancestors dancing in the sky.